RELIGION AND SAINTS

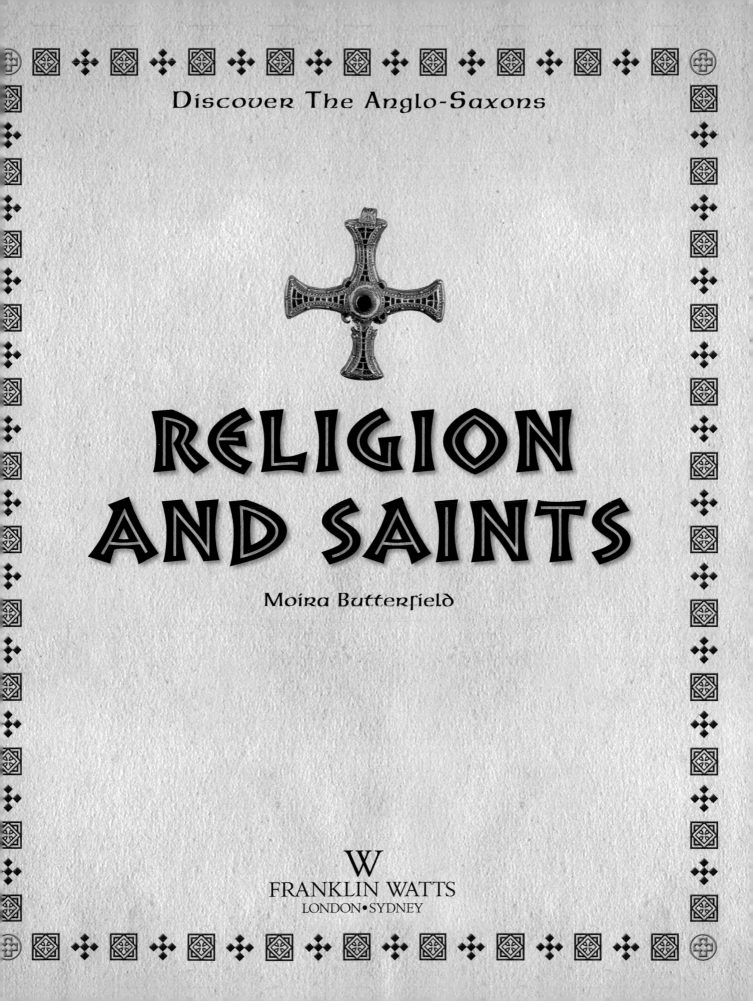

Discover The Anglo-Saxons

RELIGION AND SAINTS

Moira Butterfield

W

FRANKLIN WATTS
LONDON•SYDNEY

Franklin Watts
Published in Great Britain in 2016 by
The Watts Publishing Group

Editor in chief: John C. Miles
Series editor: Sarah Ridley
Art director: Peter Scoulding
Series designer: John Christopher/White Design
Picture research: Kathy Lockley

Dewey number: 941.01
ISBN: 978 1 4451 3339 3

Printed in China

Franklin Watts
An imprint of
Hachette Children's Group
Part of The Watts Publishing Group
Carmelite House
50 Victoria Embankment
London EC4Y 0DZ

an Hachette UK company.
www.hachette.co.uk

www.franklinwatts.co.uk

CONTENTS

ANGLO-SAXON
INVASION

For almost 400 years Britain was ruled by the ancient Romans. In 410 CE the Roman army left and new settlers began to arrive from the areas we now call Denmark, Germany and the Netherlands. We call them the Anglo-Saxons.

Gold warrior
This gold Anglo-Saxon warrior was part of the Staffordshire Hoard – an important hoard of Anglo-Saxon treasure found in 2009.

Trashed temples

The early Anglo-Saxons had no use for temples and they did not know how to build with stone. It seems they left Roman towns to fall down or built their own wooden houses amongst the old ruins.

ALL SORTS OF BELIEFS

At the time that the Romans left there were no churches as we know them today. Instead there were temples where people worshipped Roman gods and goddesses. It's thought that a few people followed Christian beliefs, and they probably gathered in their homes to worship. There were even some people who still followed ancient Celtic beliefs, worshipping their gods in sacred spots in the countryside, such as woods and pools. The new invaders were pagans who worshipped their own gods and goddesses.

A MONK'S TALE

In the 540s a monk called Gildas wrote the only account we have of what happened when the Anglo-Saxons arrived. He called the invaders "ravenous wolves" and described them smashing down old temples with battering rams, killing everyone inside and leaving bodies scattered in the street. We have no idea how true Gildas's history really is, and just how much chaos and violence the new arrivals brought. We do know that some of the native people fled to Wales, Ireland, Scotland or Brittany in France, and took their beliefs with them.

Spearmen

An illuminated manuscript from c.1130 shows Saxons, Jutes and Angles crossing the sea to England carrying shields and spears.

Legendary fightback

Gildas tells us that the Romano-Britons fought back against the invaders for a while, under the leadership of a mysterious Roman hero called Ambrosius Aurelianus. He was later called King Arthur in some early writings.

WORSHIPPED BY WARRIORS

The Anglo-Saxon invaders saw their gods and goddesses as the all-powerful givers of life and death who controlled the seasons, the weather and the Earth's fertility.

EARTH GODDESSES

Early Anglo-Saxons thought that goddesses controlled the seasons, plants and animals. Their goddesses included Nerthus (the mother of the Earth) and Eostre (the goddess of the dawn, spring and new life). There were celebrations throughout the year, including the springtime celebration for Eostre, which eventually turned into the Christian festival called Easter.

House elves

Anglo-Saxons seem to have believed in *cofgodas*, mini human spirits who helped around the house rather like elves or fairies. They also believed in magical water spirits who lived in streams and rivers.

Mystery myths

There is lots we don't know about beliefs at this time because nothing was written down. This Anglo-Saxon king's purse shows mysterious creatures and figures that nobody now understands.

WARRIOR GODS

Tir, Woden and Thunor were important Anglo-Saxon gods. Woden was the god of magic and of warriors. He was associated with war and death, and warriors made offerings to him before going into battle in the hope of gaining his protection. Early Anglo-Saxon kings claimed that they were descended from Woden, giving them a special claim to power. Tir was a war god symbolising honour and glory, and Thunor was god of the sky and of thunder. Anglo-Saxons believed in lucky charms, and warriors sometimes wore pieces of jewellery in the shape of Thunor's hammer to give them the god's protection.

Viking Thor
This little figure, which probably shows Thor and his hammer, comes from Iceland. Vikings worshipped Thor, as did the Anglo-Saxons, but they called him Thunor.

Yuletide party time

Pagan Anglo-Saxons celebrated New Year at the time when we now celebrate Christmas. They had a feast and burnt a special Yule log on the fire. The word Yule comes from *geol*, the Anglo-Saxon name for their pagan winter event.

THE POPE'S PEOPLE

A marriage between a European princess called Bertha and an English king called Aethelbert helped bring Christianity to the Anglo-Saxons. At the time there were several different kingdoms in the land. Aethelbert was ruler of the kingdom of Kent.

Angels in waiting

Legend has it that Pope Gregory I decided to send his monks to convert the Anglo-Saxons to Christianity when he saw some fair-haired slaves in a local Roman market. He was told they were pagan English settlers called 'Angles', but he said he thought they looked more like angels!

AUGUSTINE ARRIVES

By the 500s Christianity was the main religion in Europe, led by the Pope in Rome. Princess Bertha, who came from the land we now call France, was a Christian, but King Aethelbert was still a pagan. In 597 Pope Gregory I sent 40 monks from Rome to Kent, led by Augustine. The monks hoped that Bertha would persuade her husband to let them stay. At first they were nervous that their mission might be too difficult, and they nearly gave up and turned back. But the monks eventually arrived and Aethelbert agreed they could set up churches in Canterbury, the capital of his kingdom. Aethelbert soon became Christian himself.

PRAY OUR WAY

There were already some Christian monks in the north and west of Britain, members of the Celtic Church. The monks of Rome criticised them for not converting enough people and for not following the rules of worship set down by the Pope. Some even blamed them for the pagan invasion of England, calling it God's punishment for their bad behaviour. Augustine's monks took their orders from Rome and thought that the Celtic monks should do so, too.

St Martin's Church

Augustine and his 40 monks made their base at this church in 597. It now forms part of the Canterbury World Heritage Site.

TIME OF CHANGE

The Anglo-Saxon people did not convert to Christianity overnight. There were arguments and setbacks until the mid-600s. It must have been a confusing and unsettling time for people.

YES OR NO?

Around 731 an Anglo-Saxon monk called Bede wrote a history of Britain explaining what happened in early Christian times. He tells us that some Anglo-Saxon kings refused to convert and preferred to stay pagan, but King Redwald of East Anglia apparently did both! He was baptised a Christian but his wife was pagan and persuaded him to have two altars – one for each religion. Arguments about religion continued. For instance, although Bertha and Aethelbert of Kent were Christian, their son King Eadbald was pagan.

Bede's book
This illustration from the 12th century shows an Anglo-Saxon monk writing. It is thought to be Bede, who wrote an important history of early Britain.

 Kings keep fighting

Anglo-Saxon kings were tough warriors, whether Christian or pagan. For instance, King Caedwalla of Wessex attacked the Isle of Wight in 685 to wipe out the native people there. He killed the pagan king and his sons after forcing them to convert to Christianity. Then he gave conquered land to the Church.

EASTER ARGUMENT

Even within the Christian Church, arguments occurred. For instance, Celtic monks based in Scotland set the date of Easter differently to the monks from Rome. This caused a big problem because Christians were meant to fast (go without rich food) for Lent, a period of time running up to Easter. In Northumbria King Oswiu and his court fasted during Lent, then feasted on the Easter date set by the Celtic monks. Meanwhile his wife, Queen Eanfled, followed the Easter date set by the monks of Rome, which was later. She had to look on hungrily while her husband tucked into his feast. In 664 a synod (meeting of churchmen) was called at Whitby, where King Oswiu ruled that everyone should follow the Pope's rules.

Pope-style

This picture from the 1200s shows a monk having his hair cut by another monk. Their hairstyle is Roman, not Celtic.

Style wars

The Synod of Whitby didn't just argue over the date of Easter. The monks disagreed about haircuts, too. Celtic monks shaved their hair at the front but grew it long at the back. Roman monks wore their hair cut round, with a shaved patch in the middle.

ANGLO-SAXON CHURCHES

The first Christian priests preached outdoors next to stone crosses. Then churches were built, often on sites once sacred to earlier people.

St Peter's Chapel, Bradwell-on-Sea
It is said that this chapel was built in 654 by Bishop Cedd as part of a monastery that has since fallen down.

A farm font

The early churches had stone fonts where people were baptised. A few of these have survived and are still used today. An Anglo-Saxon church at Deerhurst in Gloucestershire got its font back after many centuries when it was found on a farm being used as an animal trough (see p. 26).

INSIDE ARCHES

Most Anglo-Saxons lived in wooden homes, so imagine how they would have felt walking into a stone church building for the first time! The early churches had small narrow windows, so inside it would have been shadowy, with candles flickering on religious wall carvings (see p. 27) and paintings. There might have been some fine gold-embroidered cloth on the altar, and perhaps wall-hangings, too. The church doors and archways were usually shaped with round tops.

LOVELY LOOKOUTS

It's thought that early churches might have been used for defence as well as for worship, and that could be why they were built with towers. A tower would have made a good lookout point to see enemies such as approaching Vikings (see p. 22). Many early churches have been destroyed or replaced over time, but you can still sometimes spot Anglo-Saxon church towers, windows and doors.

(see p. 22)

Lookout tower

St Peter's Church in Barton-upon-Humber still has its Anglo-Saxon tower, an excellent place for someone to spot enemies sailing up the River Humber.

Stone detectives

There were no hammers or chisels when the first churches were built. The masons had to hack the stone with axes, so the stonework around Anglo-Saxon windows and doors tends to look quite rough. It's a good clue for people who like to hunt out early Anglo-Saxon buildings.

MONKS MAKE A HOME

Monks and nuns established new Christian communities away from ordinary people. They built abbeys, monasteries or priories (smaller than abbeys), with farms and gardens attached.

16

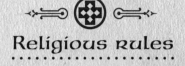

Religious rules

Rules made it clear what monks and nuns should wear: long wool tunics tied with a rope belt for monks and wool tunics and a veil for the nuns. Every monk or nun had a set rank and daily chores such as working in the garden or writing out holy books.

LIVING BY THE RULES

The monks who arrived from Rome followed the rules of Saint Benedict, which set down how monks should live every hour of the day. In Benedictine monasteries there was a strict daily timetable of chores and prayer. Monks and nuns took vows of poverty, obedience and chastity, agreeing to give up their possessions, obey their abbot or abbess and never marry.

Home for both

Monks and nuns lived in separate buildings, though sometimes within the same abbey.

WHO JOINED?

Children as young as seven could join a religious community as an 'oblate' – training to be a monk or a nun. They might be sent there because their families were too poor to look after them, or hoped that by giving their children to a monastery or convent they might get God's favour. Older people such as wealthy widows sometimes joined abbeys to live out their days in comfort and peace.

Whitby Abbey

Anglo-Saxon monks and nuns once lived in a monastery at Whitby, North Yorkshire. Later it became an important medieval abbey (below).

Holy loners

A few early religious people preferred to spend time as hermits, living on their own in remote locations. For instance, we know that an Irish monk called Kevin of Glendalough lived in a cave in the 500s, wearing only animal skins. People treated him as a wise man and went to see him to ask his advice. Later he was made a saint, and his cave is still known as Saint Kevin's Bed.

HOLY BOOKS

Some Anglo-Saxon monks spent their time writing and decorating beautiful religious books for churchmen and wealthy nobles to use.

Lindisfarne treasure
A page from the beautiful *Lindisfarne Gospels* manuscript, one of the finest objects still surviving from Anglo-Saxon times.

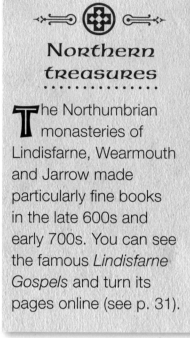

Northern treasures

The Northumbrian monasteries of Lindisfarne, Wearmouth and Jarrow made particularly fine books in the late 600s and early 700s. You can see the famous *Lindisfarne Gospels* and turn its pages online (see p. 31).

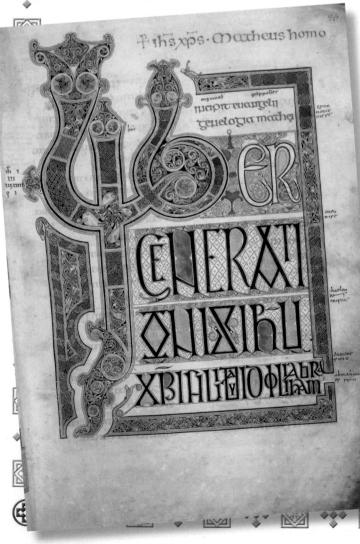

MONKS AT WORK
The monks who made manuscripts worked in a monastery area called the scriptorium. They prepared their inks by grinding plants or minerals into a paste mixed with egg white or fish glue, and they wrote on parchment made of smoothed animal skin, using pens carved from bird quills or reeds. Before they began they carefully worked out their page designs on wax tablets (wax sheets they could scratch and then wipe clean). Once finished, the pages were sewn together and bound in fine leather or ivory.

IN ENGLISH

At this time religious works were written in Latin, but the monks sometimes wrote English translations underneath the Latin lines. We call Anglo-Saxon English 'Old English'. When the monks drew pictures on manuscripts, they tended to show Bible stories re-set in Anglo-Saxon times. For instance, in the *Old English Hexateuch*, a manuscript probably made in Canterbury in the early 1000s, the characters in the Old Testament were all drawn with Anglo-Saxon clothes and haircuts.

Anglo-Saxon Noah

Noah brings in his wine harvest dressed in Anglo-Saxon clothes in this page from the *Old English Hexateuch*, probably made in Canterbury around 1000.

Ink from near and far

The inks the monks used came from many different sources. For instance, they gathered oak galls, round growths found on oak trees (right), to make brown-black ink. By contrast, blue lapis lazuli ink came from stones gathered far away in the foothills of the Himalayas!

TOP CHURCHES AND CHURCHMEN

High-ranking churchmen such as abbots, bishops and archbishops were the main advisors for kings and nobles. Abbots were based in abbeys and monasteries, while bishops and archbishops were based in cathedrals, the largest churches in the land.

Priests

Ordinary Anglo-Saxon Christians went to a small local church where a low-ranking priest ran services for them, but highborn nobles and kings had their own personal priests and private chapels.

Royal resting place
Christian Anglo-Saxon rulers were buried in important churches. For instance, Anglo-Saxon ruler King Athelstan (927-939) was buried in Malmesbury Abbey, Wiltshire. This is his tomb, later rebuilt in the 1400s.

MUDDLED BONE MYSTERY

Anglo-Saxon kings and bishops were usually buried in important cathedrals such as Winchester, Canterbury or York. For instance, we know that several Anglo-Saxon kings and bishops were laid to rest in Winchester Cathedral, including King Cnut (who died in 1035), along with his wife, Queen Emma, and his son King Harthacnut. Over the centuries these Anglo-Saxon burials were disturbed and the bones were jumbled up. Now scientists are trying to date the Winchester bones, possibly using DNA to identify which belong to the same body.

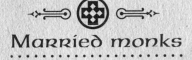

Married monks

According to the Pope's religious laws, priests were not allowed to marry. However, in Scotland churchmen followed different rules and some of them had wives. King Duncan, who ruled Scotland from 1034, had a father who was a married abbot.

Abbey treasure
This copper chalice (holy wine cup) came from an Anglo-Saxon grave at Hexham Abbey, Northumberland.

AN IMPORTANT ABBOT

We know about the lives of some Anglo-Saxon abbots and bishops from writings of the time. One of the most important was Benedict Biscop, who founded the monastery of Wearmouth in 673. Biscop travelled to Rome and brought back treasures such as books and works of art. He also brought back with him the first glaziers ever to work in England. They added glass windows to his monastery, much to everyone's amazement. He also invited an important religious music teacher from Rome, the first person to teach the English monks how to chant during services.

POWERFUL PAGANS

During the 800s pagan Vikings attacked and took over large areas of England. They stole monastery treasures and killed or captured local people, including monks, to sell as slaves in other parts of Europe.

Saint slaughter

In 867 the city of York fell to the Vikings after fierce fighting. Ivar the Boneless, the Viking king of Dublin, was the victor, and he was known for taking violent revenge on his enemies. In 869 he killed the East Anglian Christian King Edmund by tying him to a tree and shooting him full of arrows, apparently because Edmund refused to turn pagan. Later Edmund was made a saint (see p. 24).

Invaders arrive
Re-enactors recreate the warlike Vikings, who were pagan when they first arrived in Britain.

ALFRED FIGHTS BACK

At first the Vikings were so successful that Anglo-Saxon rule very nearly ended in Britain. Only Alfred, King of Wessex, held out. He managed to turn the tide by defeating Viking leader Guthrum at the Battle of Eddington in Wiltshire in 878. After the battle, Alfred forced Guthrum and his warriors to become Christians, and they signed a treaty that split the country between the Anglo-Saxons and the Vikings. Gradually, over time, the Anglo-Saxons regained territory and the Vikings converted to Christianity.

TREASURES DESTROYED

In the years before they converted to Christianity, Vikings smashed and looted monasteries and churches across the north and east of the country. They burnt many fine monastery libraries, which is why manuscripts from this time or earlier are so rare. The Vikings did not write things down, and they believed in war-like gods and goddesses, not the Christian God, so they saw no value in religious objects such as holy books. We can only guess at the many wonderful poems and beautiful pictures they must have destroyed.

A complicated CROSS

The Vikings who settled in England gradually became Christian, though for a while they seemed to mix paganism and Christianity together, at least in their art. For instance, in the 10th century a Viking carved the Halton Cross (left), now in a churchyard in Lancashire. It shows the figure of Jesus but also the pagan hero Sigurd fighting a dragon.

23

CROSS-OVER CROSS
The Halton Cross is a good example of Christian and pagan stories and images mixed up together.

SAINTS AND SHRINES

T he Anglo-Saxons believed in many saints – those they believed had the holy power to perform miracles, even after they had died. People visited shrines (places associated with the saints) to pray for miracles.

A HOLY DEATH

Saints were often martyrs – people who died for their religion. One of the most famous was Saint Edmund, a king killed by the Vikings in 869 for refusing to denounce his faith (see p. 22). They cut his head off and threw it into brambles but it was said to shout out to let everyone know where it was. Edmund's body was put into a shrine at Bury St Edmunds, which became the reputed site of many miracles.

Saint Edmund's shrine
The ruins of the abbey where St Edmund's shrine once stood lie close to St Edmundsbury Cathedral in Bury St Edmunds, Suffolk.

Saintly, not smelly

The bodies of Anglo-Saxon saints were said to stay in perfect condition, by holy miracle, years after their death. In 1539 men working for Henry VIII opened the coffin of Saint Cuthbert (see below) and were reputed to have found his body complete and undecayed more than 800 years after he had died.

POWERFUL PLACES

Anglo-Saxon Christians went on pilgrimages – journeys to holy sites. They thought they would be forgiven their sins and granted their wishes if they made the effort. They might travel to a famous local shrine or even as far away as Rome itself.

They liked to visit places where relics – the body parts of dead saints – were kept. The body parts of Saint Oswald were particularly popular. Oswald, a Christian King of Northumbria, was killed by pagans in battle in 642. Parts of his body were placed in several abbeys around the country, and were very popular with pilgrims.

25

Cross of gold

Holy sites made a lot of money from pilgrims and had fine treasures. This gold cross comes from Durham Cathedral.

Carrying round Cuthbert

Saint Cuthbert was a monk who died in 687. At first he was buried at the monastery of Lindisfarne. After miracles had occurred at his grave, he was made a saint. When Vikings attacked a hundred years later, monks carried his coffin away for safety, moving it around for several years before settling it in Durham Cathedral.

READY FOR HEAVEN

Once England was Christian, ordinary people were expected to go to their local church, where they were baptised, married and buried.

BURIAL BELIEFS

Unlike their pagan ancestors, Christians were not meant to be buried with lots of objects to take to the afterlife but it seems that some of the old beliefs still survived for a while. For instance, one of the earliest Christian burials in Britain, found near Cambridge, dates from around 650. A girl aged about 16 was buried lying on a bed, with a beautiful gold cross sewn into her clothes. She probably came from a wealthy Anglo-Saxon family, perhaps one of the first in the country to convert.

People protector
This Anglo-Saxon font stands in St Mary's Church, Deerhurst in Gloucestershire. Carved from a single piece of stone, the spirals on the outside were once said to offer babies protection against the Devil during the baptism ceremony.

Facing the right way

Christians were buried with their heads to the west and their feet to the east. The idea was that they would be facing Jesus when they rose on Judgement Day at the end of the world, as described in the Bible.

Stone carvings

You can still see Anglo-Saxon stone carvings at Holy Rood Church, Daglingworth in Gloucestershire – the same carvings that locals would have seen when they went to church a thousand years ago. This one shows Saint Peter carrying the key to Heaven.

Pagan burial pots

Pagan Anglo-Saxons were sometimes cremated (burnt after death). Their ashes were buried in clay pots decorated with patterns and symbols.

VILLAGE VOICE

Most ordinary Anglo-Saxon Christians would not have been able to read a Bible. They could only listen as their local priest told them what it said. The priest was an important local person and people went to him for advice and help. Every year he collected a tithe – a payment of crops or money – from each of the people in his parish to help run the church.

A NEW RULER

Anglo-Saxon rule came to an end in 1066 when Harold, the last Anglo-Saxon king, was killed at the Battle of Hastings. A new ruler, William of Normandy, was crowned in the newly-rebuilt church of Westminster Abbey in London.

28

Harold's coronation
King Harold was crowned King of England on 6 January 1066, as shown on this part of the Bayeux Tapestry. Later that year, William of Normandy would invade England.

Picture of power
A giant embroidered picture, the Bayeux Tapestry, was made to celebrate William's victory. It shows the funeral of King Edward the Confessor, King Harold's coronation and William's invasion. It also shows a comet shooting through the sky. It appeared at the time when Harold was crowned, and people thought it was an omen that disaster was ahead!

NEW-STYLE ROYAL CHURCH

Westminster Abbey was once a small community of monks on a marshy island by the River Thames. King Edward the Confessor (ruled 1042-1066) had the site rebuilt as a much grander palace and abbey, in a new style called Romanesque – with round stone arches, stone pillars and vaulted ceilings (ceilings that look as if they have ribs). Edward died in January 1066 and was buried in Westminster Abbey. It is still the church where British kings and queens are crowned or buried.

CURIOUS CROWNING

William, Duke of Normandy, was crowned in Westminster Abbey on Christmas Day, 1066. The ceremony nearly went badly wrong when the English nobles gave him a loud traditional shout of approval. William's soldiers heard the noise outside and thought a fight had begun. They began burning houses and scuffles broke out. Inside, William is said to have trembled with fear as Archbishop Eldred put the crown on his head.

29

Westminster Abbey
The church where British monarchs have been crowned since the end of the Anglo-Saxon era. The front and towers you can see today were built much later than Anglo-Saxon times.

Place for a palace

Today's Houses of Parliament are on the site of Edward the Confessor's old palace in London. They are still called the Palace of Westminster.

GLOSSARY

Abbey A religious community of more than 14 monks or nuns. Monasteries are smaller religious communities.

Abbot The head of an abbey.

Afterlife Belief in a life after death.

Baptised Confirmed as a Christian in an official ceremony.

Benedictine A daily timetable of prayer in a monastery, written by an early monk called Saint Benedict.

Celtic beliefs Beliefs people held in Britain in ancient times, before Roman, Anglo-Saxon pagan or Christian times.

Christianity Belief in the God of the Holy Bible.

Cofgodas Mini human spirits believed to help around the Anglo-Saxon house.

Conversion Changing from one religion to another.

Deities Gods and goddesses.

Eostre Early Anglo-Saxon goddess of the spring.

Illumination Decoration painted onto a manuscript.

Lent A period of time before Easter, when Christians are supposed to fast (have much less food and drink than normal).

Manuscript A handwritten document.

Martyr Someone who died because of their religion.

Monk A religious man who lives in a monastery and devotes his life to God.

Nerthus An Anglo-Saxon goddess thought of as the mother of the Earth.

Nun A religious woman who lives in an abbey or convent.

ANGLO-SAXON TIMELINE

410 CE The Roman army leaves Britain.

449 The Angles and Saxons arrive by boat in south-east Britain. The Britons fight to push them back.

540 The invading Angles, Saxons and Jutes conquer England. They are pagan, not Christian.

563 Irish monk Columba founds a Christian monastery on the island of Iona.

585 By now seven separate kingdoms have formed in England – Mercia, East Anglia, Northumbria, Essex, Wessex, Sussex and Kent.

Each has their own king. Over time, some kings become *bretwalda* – overlords of the other kings.

597 Aethelbert, King of Kent, becomes the first Anglo-Saxon Christian leader, converted by the monk Augustine. Gradually others convert to Christianity.

620 (approx) The death and burial of an East Anglian king (probably Redwald) at Sutton Hoo in Suffolk.

664 A meeting at Whitby decides between Celtic Christianity and the Christianity of Rome. The Christianity of Rome is preferred.

731 A monk called Bede finishes writing a history of Britain, the best source of history we have about this time.

789 The first recorded Viking attack on the British Isles, at Portland in Dorset.

793 Vikings attack the monastery at Lindisfarne.

865 A big Viking force, the Great Heathen Army, arrives and rampages across the country for the next 14 years.

878 Alfred, King of Wessex, defeats Danish Vikings at the Battle of Edington. The Danes and the Anglo-Saxons agree to split England between them.

Old English The name we give to the language written and spoken by the Anglo-Saxons.

Paganism Belief in many gods and goddesses.

Pilgrimage A journey made to a holy place.

Pope The leader of the Catholic Church, based in Rome.

Relic The remains of a saint or a holy object.

Romanesque A type of church architecture.

Sacred Something that is believed to be connected magically to God.

Scriptorium Part of a monastery where manuscript writing was done.

Synod A meeting of churchmen.

Thunor Anglo-Saxon god of the sky and of thunder.

Tir Anglo-Saxon god symbolising honour and glory.

Woden Anglo-Saxon god of magic and warriors.

899 Alfred dies. He is succeeded as King of Wessex by his son, Edward.

911 Alfred's daughter Aethelflaed takes over the rule of Mercia after the death of her husband.

937 Athelstan, King of Wessex and Mercia, defeats an army of Vikings and Scots at the Battle of Brunanburh. He then rules over the whole of England.

1016 Danish King Cnut becomes King of England, deposing Ethelred the Unready. Anglo-Danish kings rule England for a while.

1042 Edward, son of Ethelred the Unready, takes power. Brought up in Normandy, he apparently promised his throne to his great-nephew, William, when he died.

1066 Harold Godwinson is chosen as king but reigns for only ten months. The Anglo-Saxons are defeated by William, Duke of Normandy, at the Battle of Hastings.

www.regia.org/research/church/church1.htm
Find out how scribes made illuminated manuscripts.

www.bl.uk/onlinegallery/ttp/lindisfarne/accessible/introduction.html#content
Hear an audio introduction to the *Lindisfarne Gospels* and turn the pages online. You can also explore the pages of the *Old English Hexateuch*.

www.earlybritishkingdoms.com/adversaries/bios/
A long list of Anglo-Saxon saints and their stories.

http://anglosaxondiscovery.ashmolean.org/teachers_resources/activities.html
Anglo-Saxon activity sheets.

http://www.youtube.com/watch?annotation_id=annotation_559561&feature=iv&src_vid=bDaB-NNyM8o&v=LtGoBZ4D4_E
See an animated (moving) section of the Bayeux Tapestry.

31

INDEX